BY CHIARA PIRODDI

ILLUSTRATED BY FEDERICA FUSI

A FIRST BOOK OF MINDFULNESS FOR KIDS

WSKIDS
WHITE STAR KIDS

Dragon Fruit

INTRODUCTION (FOR PARENTS)

HAVE YOU EVER NOTICED THAT SOMETIMES OUR MINDS ARE LIKE BUSY HIGHWAYS WITHOUT ANY RULES OR REGULATIONS?

Thoughts stream in from all directions, with appointments and worries overtaking our focus and speeding away before we know what's happening. We turn on autopilot and launch ourselves into the chaos, but when will there be time to reflect on what really matters?

MINDFULNESS IS AN APPROACH THAT HELPS TEACH US TO MANAGE THIS MENTAL AND PHYSICAL OVERLOAD BY STAYING IN THE PRESENT MOMENT.

It makes us more aware of our internal world, which is made up of thoughts, emotions, and physical sensations.

By learning how we can adopt a compassionate, nonjudgmental attitude toward ourselves and the people around us, we can calm our fears of the past and our anxieties about the future.

ARE CHILDREN UP TO THE CHALLENGE?

Actually, adults have a lot to learn from children! Their free, instinctive, and receptive minds naturally live in the present. Thus it's quite easy to teach them how to develop their mindfulness. The exercises in this book are presented as games. Children take part simply by using THEIR BREATH, BODY, AND IMAGINATION.

The exercises can be done alone or with the whole family. Participants are encouraged to share the sensations they feel after each exercise is complete. In a warm, relaxing tone, read the instructions for each exercise aloud.

Don't be in a hurry to achieve results.
Allow your children to do the exercises in ways that feel comfortable to them.

Doing these exercises every day can help teach children how to calm down in emotional moments, how to be patient and use their concentration skills, and how to develop an open and creative mind.

Let Pam and Sam lead the way. These siblings are very different from each other, but they both share a passion for the pursuit of mindfulness. Together with their dog Happy, they will be your mindfulness guides.

IN THE PAGES THAT FOLLOW, YOU'LL FIND MANY FUN, RELAXING EXERCISES FOR THE MORNING, THE AFTERNOON, AND RIGHT BEFORE BEDTIME.

Breath after breath, this journey will lead you and your children toward a more mindful existence. Discover the harmony between the outside world and the world inside our own heads!

BEFORE WE START...

PAM

SAM

SAM: "That's it. I give up!"

PAM: "What's wrong?"

SAM: "Chores, chores, and more chores! I feel like my brain's going to explode!"

PAM: "I think I know how to help! Have I ever told you about MINDFULNESS?"

SAM: "MIND...what? What are you talking about, Pam?"

PAM: "Let's start by BREATHING. This is the secret to becoming more mindful."

SAM: "But I get bored sitting down! And I breathe all the time. See? I'm doing it right now. What's so special about it?"

PAM: "This time you're only going to think about your breathing as you draw in each new breath."

SAM: "But that's impossible, my head is full of thoughts! How can I focus on just one?"

PAM: "Our heads are always full of thoughts, but if we make the effort, we can teach our minds to only focus on one thing at a time. Let's try it together! Take a deep breath. Okay, now count each new breath that you take."

SAM: "One... two... three..." (breathes)

PAM: "Good. How's your head feeling now?"

SAM: "Hmmm, I think it feels a little better! Thanks, Pam! Now I feel like my thoughts are walking instead of running."

"HOORAY! WELCOME TO MINDFULNESS!"

...LET'S LEARN HOW TO BREATHE!

FIND A COMFORTABLE POSITION TO SIT IN. TAKE YOUR TIME. FEEL YOUR FEET TOUCHING THE FLOOR. Are you comfortable? Are your legs relaxed? Keep your back straight. Are your shoulders relaxed? Your eyes can be open or closed, whichever you prefer. PUT ONE HAND ON YOUR CHEST AND THE OTHER ON YOUR BELLY. FEEL THE HEAT OF YOUR HANDS ON YOUR BODY.

BREATHE SLOWLY, THERE'S NO HURRY.

Can you feel the air entering your nostrils? It travels down to your lungs and gently inflates them. Your chest slowly rises. Your belly fills with air, like a balloon. Welcome, air!

Now, let the air return to the world. Open your mouth slightly, forming a small O. Can you feel the air leaving? Can you feel your chest falling? Your belly is now empty, small, and soft.

THANK YOU, AIR, FOR FILLING ME WITH CALMNESS!

NOW, LET'S REPEAT
THE EXERCISE LYING DOWN.
FIND A SMALL, PLUSH TOY OR
STUFFED ANIMAL.

Lie down with your back straight. It should be touching
the ground. Put the stuffed animal on top of your belly.
"Are you ready, little one? Now, let's learn to surf the waves!"

When you're ready, start breathing.
Breathe in through your nostrils.
Feel your belly filling with air. UP UP UP!
Feel your stuffed animal rising higher and higher.
Now it's on the crest of the wave.

Slowly exhale. DOWN DOWN DOWN!
Feel your belly slowly becoming empty. Your stuffed animal
is coming back down, riding the wave back into the water.

Repeat this breathing exercise 3 times.
THERE'S NO HURRY!

How do you feel after breathing like this?

EACH TIME YOU SEE THIS SYMBOL,
TRY THIS NEW BREATHING
TECHNIQUE YOU'VE LEARNED!

GOOD MORNING, WORLD!

Hooray, a new day awaits! Let's open the window to the world. Look at the light and the colors. Smell the fragrances! Now, let's open ourselves to the world and welcome it inside with confidence. Whenever we do this, we prepare ourselves for whatever adventures and challenges each day holds!

THE SCENT OF AWAKENING

(EXERCISE TO LEARN HOW TO BREATHE IN DEEPLY. USEFUL FOR ACTIVATING THE BODY)

WE GREET THE NEW DAY BY BREATHING TOGETHER,
JUST LIKE WE LEARNED ON THE PREVIOUS PAGE.
LET'S DO IT 3 TIMES SLOWLY.

Here's the first flower. What does it smell like?. Inhale deeply
for 5 seconds. Capture the flower's scent. CAN YOU FEEL
ITS SCENT ENTERING YOUR NOSTRILS? HOW DOES IT SMELL?
Now, exhale the air naturally, making it last for 2 seconds.

Now, smell another flower. Smell as many flowers
as you like!. Breathe in deeply and exhale the air
naturally. HOW DO YOU FEEL AFTER SMELLING
ALL THOSE FLOWERS?

THE AWAKENING OF THE HIPPOPOTAMUS

(EXERCISE TO AWAKEN THE FACE MUSCLES)

THE HIPPOPOTAMUS HAS JUST WOKEN UP.
YAWN ALONG WITH IT!

YAAAAWN! Open your mouth wide. Show all your teeth, just like the hippopotamus below. Feel your jaw move as your mouth opens and closes!

Another big YAAAAWN!
Feel how your face muscles pull when you open and close your mouth. Once more. YAAAAWN!

OH! THAT WAS A SPONTANEOUS YAWN! WELCOME, YAWN!

HOW DOES YOUR BODY FEEL AFTER ALL THAT YAWNING?

AGILE LIKE A DOLPHIN

(EXERCISE TO AWAKEN THE BODY BY MOVING AND BREATHING IN DEEPLY)

STAND WITH YOUR ARMS AT YOUR SIDES AND YOUR BACK STRAIGHT. BREATHE.
THE DOLPHIN HAS ARRIVED! WE'RE GOING TO SWIM LIKE HE DOES!

Breathe in as much air as possible. Now, go underwater!
Feel the water around you. Is it cold or warm?

Stretch out your neck.
Shrug your shoulders up. Relax your shoulders.
Shrug your shoulders again. Relax your shoulders.
Now, stick your head out of the water.
BREATHE OUT ALL THE AIR.

Hold your breath.
Rotate your shoulders
backward. Rotate your
shoulders forward.
Swim back to the
surface. BREATHE
OUT ALL THE AIR.

Hold your breath. Tilt
your pelvis backward and
forward. Tilt backward
and forward. BREATHE
OUT ALL THE AIR.

HOW DOES YOUR BODY FEEL NOW?

AS STRONG AS A GORILLA

(EXERCISE TO AWAKEN THE BODY AND FEEL MORE SECURE)

AWAKEN YOUR INNER GORILLA!

Close your eyes and breathe. We are in the jungle, surrounded by tall, green plants covered in tropical flowers. All around us are beautiful, colorful parrots. Open your eyes and breathe. Picture a family of gorillas. Now, imagine that YOU ARE ONE OF THEM!

Stand up and stretch your arms out to your sides. Stretch them as far as you can, leaving your hands wide open. BREATHE IN. Straighten your shoulders. Lift your neck and head up. EXHALE.

Push your chest out as far as it will go. Breathe in. Shout: "I am as strong as a gorilla!" Breathe out all the air while beating your fists against your chest. Boom, boom, boom!

Push your chest out as far as it will go again. Breathe in. Shout: "I am as strong as a gorilla!" Breathe out all the air while stomping your feet on the ground. Stomp, stomp, stomp!

Once more, push your chest out as far as it will go. Breathe in. Shout: "I am as strong as a gorilla!" Breathe out all the air while beating your fists against your chest and stomping your feet. Boom, stomp, boom, stomp!

CONCENTRATE ON THIS THOUGHT:
"I AM AS STRONG AS A GORILLA."
HOW DOES IT MAKE YOU FEEL?

POSITIVE THOUGHTS IN YOUR POCKET

(SELF-ESTEEM BUILDING EXERCISE INTENDED FOR THE WHOLE FAMILY)

THERE'S NO HURRY THIS MORNING.

Let's all have breakfast together! Okay, now we each get a pen and as many slips of paper as there are family members. On each of our slips of paper, we draw a symbol or write a word or a phrase that we want to dedicate to each member of our family.

We fold the slips of paper and give them to each of the people we made them for. Make sure to look each person in the eye as you give them their slip of paper.

How do you feel after drawing or writing these notes?

NOW IT'S YOUR TURN! OPEN YOUR HANDS AND RECEIVE ALL THE POSITIVE THOUGHTS AND DRAWINGS FROM YOUR FAMILY! HOW DO YOU FEEL AFTER RECEIVING THESE NOTES?

DON'T FORGET TO PUT THEM IN YOUR POCKET! THAT WAY YOU WILL ALWAYS HAVE THEM WITH YOU. DURING DIFFICULT MOMENTS, YOU CAN TAKE THEM OUT AND READ THEM!

A BACKPACK FULL OF HUGS

(EXERCISE TO DO WITH YOUR FAMILY WHEN YOU NEED A LITTLE COMFORT)

YOU SHOULD NEVER LEAVE YOUR HOUSE WITHOUT A SUPPLY OF HUGS!

Let's stand in a circle together and all take a deep breath.

Everybody should move closer. Let's take turns hugging each other. If we want to, we can hug more than once!

As we hug, let's take a deep breath together. While you're doing this, imagine putting that hug in your backpack.

Hold your breath.
Tilt your pelvis backward and forward.
Backward and forward.
BREATHE OUT ALL THE AIR.

DO YOU WANT
MORE HUGS, OR
ARE YOU READY TO
GO OUTSIDE NOW?

NEW ADVENTURES AWAIT!

AFTERNOON
(HALFWAY THROUGH THE JOURNEY)

Gosh, I've had to sit still for hours, concentrating and being careful of what I say and do. I got bored a lot. Sometimes I felt as though there was a heavy weight pushing against my shoulders and forehead.

　　Hmmm, what's this stormy sea stirring in my belly? Why are my hands sweating? And why do my feet feel like they want to run?

　　I think my exhausting day is starting to catch up with me. Let's focus on ourselves. We'll learn how to manage the waves of our most overwhelming emotions. With a little practice, our minds can be taught to ride these unpredictable waves.

REMEMBER
TO START EACH
EXERCISE WITH
A DEEP BREATH.

TAKE YOUR TIME
AND RELAX.

A RAY OF SUNSHINE FOR ME

(EXERCISE FOR BETTER SELF-AWARENESS)

HEY, WHERE ARE YOU GOING IN SUCH A HURRY?
STOP FOR A MINUTE AND ENJOY THIS RAY OF SUNSHINE!

Stand up, close your eyes, and tilt your face up. Imagine standing on a beautiful beach and feeling the warmth of the sunshine on your face. Ahh, it's so warm! BREATHE.

Now, imagine the sunshine wrapping itself around you like a golden thread. Feel the heat gradually enveloping your body.

Look at the golden thread around your head and neck. BREATHE.

Now, look at the thread around your shoulders. It's flowing down your arms and hands. How do your hands feel? BREATHE.

The golden thread goes around your chest, then onto your belly. BREATHE. Do you feel the warmth?

Now it's wrapping itself around your legs, your knees, your calves, and your feet. Mmmm, feel how warm your feet are! BREATHE.

HOW DOES YOUR BODY FEEL BEING EMBRACED BY THE SUN? ARE THERE ANY PARTS OF YOUR BODY YOU WOULD LIKE TO BE EMBRACED BY THE SUN AGAIN?

BUTTERFLIES OF FREEDOM

(IMAGINATIVE EXERCISE TO FREE YOURSELF FROM WORRIES)

ARE THERE TOO MANY THOUGHTS IN YOUR HEAD?
LET'S GIVE SOME TO OUR FRIENDS, THE BUTTERFLIES!

While you're breathing in, a butterfly flies toward you.
WHAT DOES IT LOOK LIKE? While you exhale, you give it one of
your thoughts. Fly away, butterfly, and take this thought with
you! BREATHE AND WATCH THE BUTTERFLY AS IT FLIES AWAY.

Move on to your next thought.
Breathe in. Another butterfly is coming. WHAT
DOES IT LOOK LIKE? Now, exhale and give
a thought to the second butterfly.

AHH, ONE LESS THOUGHT!

BREATHE AND WATCH
THE BUTTERFLY
AS IT FLIES AWAY.
HOW DOES IT FEEL TO
WATCH YOUR THOUGHTS
FLY AWAY?

THE LION'S ROAR

(EXERCISE TO BRING OUT COURAGE DURING MOMENTS OF INSECURITY)

HEY, WHY ARE YOU LOOKING SO DEFEATED?
SIT DOWN AND BREATHE!

Drum on your knees with your fingers.
Can you feel the lion's claws?
BREATHE.

Stomp your feet fast on the ground.
Can you feel the strength
of the lion's paws? BREATHE.

Now, take a deep breath. Put your arms above your head.
While doing this, exhale and make a roaring sound, like this:
ROOAAAARRR!

Again. Breathe. Arms above the head. And now roar:
ROOAAAARRR!

Once more:
ROOAAAARRR!

I'M AS STRONG
AS A LION!

DINNERTIME!

(EXERCISE TO DEVELOP AWARENESS OF FLAVORS
AND THE FEELING OF HUNGER)

IS IT TIME TO EAT YET? I HEARD MY BELLY GROWLING!

Sit down and put your hands on your belly.
BREATHE.

Feel the air filling up your belly.
Imagine opening a door to your belly. Wow!
There's a big table in there! Let's set it together.
BREATHE.

Bring your plate,
your fork, your glass,
and your napkin.
BREATHE.

Now, what kind of food would you like to serve at your table?
Some pasta? A loaf of bread? Maybe some fruit?
Listen to what your belly would like.
BREATHE.

Yummy! What does the food smell
like? What does it look like?
BREATHE.

Now, sit down and start eating.
Take a mouthful of food. Chew it thoroughly. Move your jaw
and your tongue. When you're ready, swallow the food.
Taste the flavor. Is it sweet or salty? Is it spicy?
Feel the texture of the food in your mouth. Is it rough or creamy?
BREATHE.

Chew more of your food.
How does your mouth feel?
How does
your belly feel?

TRY DOING THIS
EXERCISE WHILE
YOU ARE ACTUALLY
EATING! CLOSE
YOUR EYES,
BREATHE, AND
CONCENTRATE ON
EVERY MOUTHFUL
OF FOOD THAT YOU
CHEW. HOW DOES
IT FEEL?

HOORAY FOR ME!

(EXERCISE TO PRACTICE POSITIVE INTERNAL DIALOGUE)

HAVE YOU EVER BEEN AFRAID TO DO SOMETHING?
LET'S CHEER YOU ON TOGETHER!

SIT DOWN AND BREATHE.
Close your eyes and imagine that there is a person sitting in front of you. Maybe there are even two or three people sitting there! The people you see love and care about you. BREATHE.

These people are here for you! They look at you and smile. BREATHE.

"Everything is going to be okay!" they tell you. BREATHE.

Now, think the same thing: "Everything is going to be okay! Everything is going to be okay!" BREATHE.

HOW
DO YOU FEEL
NOW?

A CALMING CUP OF TEA

(EXERCISE TO CREATE A CALM INNER FEELING)

DOES IT FELL LIKE THERE'S A STORMY SEA IN YOUR BELLY?
DON'T WORRY, LET'S HAVE A CUP OF TEA!

SIT DOWN AND BREATHE.
Imagine looking at your stormy sea. It's outside the window of your bedroom, but fortunately you are sitting safely on your bed. The waves are what you're worried about, as they keep appearing one after the other!

Pick up your cup of tea. Be careful, it's very hot.
Breathe in and then blow hard on the cup.
Now, take a sip! Feel the warm calmness. It travels down your throat and into your belly, warming your heart as it goes.

Blow on the cup again
and take another sip.
With each sip of tea,
the waves will help
calm you down.

mmmm... BREATHE.
FEEL HOW WARM
YOUR BELLY
IS NOW?

Sip your tea until the
whole cup is finished.

LOOK OUT
THE WINDOW!
THE SEA IS CALM
AND PEACEFUL AGAIN!

THE CHIMPANZEE DANCE

(A SIMPLE SEQUENCE OF MOVEMENTS TO STIMULATE CONCENTRATION, SELF-CONTROL, MEMORY, AND BODY AWARENESS)

DO YOU FEEL TIRED OR UNFOCUSED AFTER SITTING
FOR TOO MANY HOURS? THEN LET'S DANCE!

Stand up and breathe. Get your mind ready
to follow the movements below, one after
the other:

SOLE OF THE FOOT. PALM OF THE HAND.
SOLE OF THE FOOT. PALM OF THE HAND.
SCRATCH YOUR ARMPITS.
SCRATCH YOUR ARMPITS.
SHAKE YOUR SHOULDERS.
SHAKE YOUR HANDS.
PULL YOUR CHEEKS.
THEN JUMP AS HIGH AS YOU CAN!

TAKE 3 DEEP BREATHS
AND DO IT AGAIN!

SOLE OF THE FOOT. PALM OF THE HAND.
SOLE OF THE FOOT. PALM OF THE HAND.
SCRATCH YOUR ARMPITS.
SCRATCH YOUR ARMPITS.
SHAKE YOUR SHOULDERS.
SHAKE YOUR HANDS.
PULL YOUR CHEEKS.
THEN JUMP AS HIGH AS YOU CAN!

BREATHE.
DO IT AGAIN!
SOLE OF THE FOOT. PALM OF THE HAND.
SOLE OF THE FOOT. PALM OF THE HAND.
SCRATCH YOUR ARMPITS.
SCRATCH YOUR ARMPITS.
SHAKE YOUR SHOULDERS.
SHAKE YOUR HANDS.
PULL YOUR CHEEKS.
THEN JUMP AS HIGH AS YOU CAN!

HOW DO YOU FEEL
AFTER THIS DANCE?

DON'T WORRY IF YOU
DO THE MOVEMENTS
IN THE WRONG
ORDER. JUST HAVE
FUN WITH THEM!

A CAREFUL ARTIST

(EXERCISE TO STIMULATE CONCENTRATION, SELECTIVE VISUAL ATTENTION, AND VISUAL MEMORY)

PLAY THIS GAME WHEN YOUR MIND IS ALL JUMBLED.

Look at the beautiful flower on this page. Look at all its amazing details and admire its pretty colors. Take all the time you need to look at it.

BREATHE.
Now, try to draw the flower on a piece of paper. Try to do it only using your memory. BE AS DETAILED AS POSSIBLE!

When you've finished, look at the flower here and compare it to your drawing. What details did you get right? Is there anything missing?

Now, do the exercise again. Did you get more details the second time?

Play the game again. This time, use an object from where you live..

TRAIN YOUR VISUAL MEMORY AND CONCENTRATION!

HANDS IN YOUR POCKETS

(EXERCISE TO IMPROVE FOCUS AND TOUCH AWARENESS)

ARE YOUR POCKETS ALWAYS FULL?

Stand up, close your eyes, and breathe.
Open your right hand and put it into your right pocket.
What does your hand feel in there? BREATHE.

Take your time and describe everything
you feel. If you find any objects in your
pocket, try to identify them.

Breathe and put your left hand into your
left pocket. What do you feel in there?
Take your hands out and hold
them at your sides.

HOW DO YOUR HANDS FEEL NOW?

LET IT FALL AWAY

(EXERCISE FOR LETTING GO OF BUILT-UP ANGER AND TENSION)

WE ALL GET ANGRY. DON'T BE SCARED, YOU CAN HANDLE IT!
ANGER IS A USEFUL AND IMPORTANT EMOTION, BUT AFTER
ITS MOMENT HAS PASSED, IT'S TIME TO LET IT GO!

Stand up with your back straight.
TAKE A DEEP BREATH.
Clench your fists. Harder! Even harder!
EXHALE SLOWLY.
Open your hands. Do they feel different?

Now, shake your hands
as if you were shaking off
big red drops of anger.

SHAKE,
SHAKE,
SHAKE!

Watch the drops of anger fall off your
hands. Look how big and red they are!
PLOP, PLOP, PLOP.
PLOP, PLOP, PLOP.
PLOP, PLOP, PLOP.
BREATHE.

HOW DO YOU FEEL NOW
THAT YOU'VE LET GO
OF YOUR ANGER?

MY HAVEN

(EXERCISE TO RESTORE INNER CALM AND A SENSE OF SAFETY)

PSSST... DO YOU NEED AN ESCAPE FROM YOUR WORRIES? LET'S MAKE YOU A HAVEN!

SIT DOWN, CLOSE YOUR EYES, AND BREATHE.

Imagine that you can become really, really small...as small as a mouse!
You're quick and fast. Now, imagine sneaking out of the room without anyone noticing you.
BREATHE.

The door closes behind you. Ahh, all your worries are closed inside the other room.
YOU ESCAPED! NOW BREATHE.

Where did you escape to? Imagine the most beautiful place you've ever seen; a place
where you feel happy, carefree, and protected. This is where you are now.
What can you see? What can you hear?
How does it smell there?
BREATHE.

YOU CAN STAY IN YOUR HAVEN AS LONG AS YOU LIKE!

AFTERWARD, DRAW YOUR HAVEN SO YOU CAN GO BACK THERE WHENEVER YOU WANT!

BAD MOOD CLOUDS

(EXERCISE TO MANAGE EMOTIONS THAT PUT YOU IN A BAD MOOD)

BAD DAY, HUH?
IMAGINE YOU HAVE THE POWER TO CONTROL THE WIND!
NOW SIT DOWN AND BREATHE.

You are the strongest and bravest superhero around, and you're sitting calmly at the top of a high mountain.

BREATHE.
Can you feel all that air in your chest?

A cloud appears!
What does it look like?
Is it big or small? Black or blue? Which emotion does it contain? Anger, sadness, disappointment, embarrassment?

Don't let it get close to you.
Take a deep breath and blow hard.
WHOOOOSH, blow the cloud away!
You are stronger than the cloud!

There's another cloud coming!
What's this one like?
Which emotion does it contain?
Take another deep breath
and blow it as far away
as you can!

DO IT AGAIN!
WHOOOOSH!
DON'T BE AFRAID.
YOU CAN BLOW
ALL YOUR BAD
MOODS AWAY.

IT'S NIGHTTIME NOW.
SEE YOU TOMORROW,
WORLD!

Phew, what a busy day!
We've felt so many emotions!
It's time to let them go.

LET'S GET READY
TO SLEEP!

Relax your body, unload your
mind, and open your heart.
Lets be thankful for this
amazing day filled with
new experiences!

THIS WILL HELP US GET
A GOOD NIGHT'S SLEEP!

WAVE AFTER WAVE

(IMAGINATIVE EXERCISE TO RELAX THE BODY AND RELIEVE STRESS AND WORRIES)

A PRETEND BATH IS JUST WHAT WE NEED!

Lie down on your bed. Make sure your back is flat against the mattress. Put your arms at your sides. Relax your legs and feet. Take a deep breath and then exhale for 5 seconds (you can count with your fingers). Let all the air out!

Imagine you're lying in a pool of warm water. Can you feel the water against your skin? BREATHE.

Open your arms. Open your legs. Let yourself be carried away by the gentle waves in the water. BREATHE.

Up. Down. Up. Down. Slow, tiny movements. Can you feel the waves moving? Let all your stress flow into the waves. BREATHE.

LET THE WAVES CARRY YOUR STRESS AWAY!

COLORFUL BUBBLES

(EXERCISE TO CALM THE MIND)

SIT OR LIE DOWN. THEN BREATHE.

An enormous blue soap bubble is floating toward you.
Watch how it moves gently through the air.
Concentrate on its color: pale blue, just like the sky.
BREATHE.

Let the bubble surround you.
Let your mind turn blue.
BREATHE IN THE COLOR BLUE.

Here comes another bubble.
Concentrate on its color:
light green, just like a leaf.

Let the bubble surround you.
Let your mind turn green.
BREATHE IN THE
COLOR GREEN.

Let your thoughts
turn blue
and green.

HOW DO FEEL NOW
THAT YOUR MIND
IS COLORFUL?

TURN THE LIGHTS OFF

(BREATHING EXERCISE TO HELP RELAX THE BODY)

IT'S TIME TO TURN THE LIGHTS OFF!

Sit in a comfortable position. Close your eyes.
Your bedroom is filled with candles. Blow them out one at a time.
Allow the light from the moon and the stars to enter the room.

Take a short breath and slowly blow out the first
candle. Feel the air passing slowly through your lips.
Watch the flame as it goes out.

Blow out the second candle.
Feel the air passing slowly
through your lips.

THERE ARE
LOTS OF STARS
IN THE SKY
TO KEEP YOU
COMPANY.

ROCKING TO SLEEP

(EXERCISE FOR DEEP RELAXATION)

Sit down and put your head between your knees. Let your arms hang at your sides. Make sure you're comfortable! NOW BREATHE.

ROCK TO THE RIGHT.   ROCK TO THE LEFT.
TAKE A DEEP BREATH IN.   EXHALE COMPLETELY.

SHUSH!
NIGHT-NIGHT!

A COMFORTING THOUGHT

(EXERCISE TO CREATE A FEELING OF SERENITY WHILE FALLING ASLEEP)

Sit in a comfortable position on your bed. Make sure your back is straight. Take a deep breath, then count to 5 as you exhale.

Think about a person or animal you love and enjoy being with. KEEP BREATHING. Take long, slow breaths. HOW DO YOU FEEL WHEN YOU THINK ABOUT THIS PERSON OR ANIMAL?

Put a hand over your heart. Think about how grateful you are to have such a wonderful person or animal in your life.

Now, draw a picture of you with them. You could draw a picture of the two of you hugging, holding hands, or playing together.

WHEN YOU'VE FINISHED, CUT OUT YOUR DRAWING AND STICK IT TO THE WALL ABOVE YOUR BED. EVERY NIGHT, YOU'LL FALL ASLEEP REMEMBERING HOW GRATEFUL YOU ARE.

WE CAN'T CONTROL THE SEA, BUT WE CAN AT LEAST RIDE THE WAVES

HERE ARE SOME PHRASES TO READ AND REMEMBER WHEN YOU WANT TO FEEL CALM AND SAFE DURING THE DAY.

I'LL HOLD ON TIGHTLY TO THIS MORNING'S SMILE ALL DAY LONG.

JUST LIKE A TREE LETTING ITS LEAVES FALL, I CAN LET GO OF MY SAD THOUGHTS AND ANGRY EMOTIONS.

WHEN I FEEL AGITATED, I CAN BREATHE, AND EVERYTHING WILL SEEM LESS DIFFICULT.

I AM WONDERFUL JUST AS I AM BECAUSE I AM THE ONLY ME IN THE WORLD.

THANK YOU FOR WHO I AM!

MY FAMILY'S LOVE WILL BE WITH ME ALL DAY LONG.

BREATHE. MY PROBLEMS WILL SOON PASS, AND I'LL FEEL SAFE AGAIN.

NO MATTER WHERE I AM, I'M SAFE INSIDE MY FAMILY'S THOUGHTS.

WHO DO I WANT TO HELP TODAY?
THANK YOU, SUN, FOR RETURNING TO LIGHT UP MY DAY.
DON'T BE IN A HURRY. BE PATIENT!
I AM THE BEST FRIEND THAT I COULD EVER ASK FOR.
CALMNESS AND TRANQUILITY ARE MY MIND'S FRIENDS. THEY HELP ME CONCENTRATE.
MY HEART IS FULL OF KINDNESS FOR OTHERS.
IT DOESN'T MATTER IF I MAKE A MISTAKE. EVERY MISTAKE IS AN OPPORTUNITY TO LEARN AND GROW.
BREATHE. LET WORRIES OUT AND CALMNESS IN.

CHIARA PIRODDI is a psychologist specializing in pediatric neuropsychology and child and adolescent psychotherapy. She has always been interested in the study and application of a bottom-up approach to body therapies, and she has cultivated her interest in mindfulness in both her private life and her profession. Her work mainly revolves around adolescents, young adults, and offering parenting support. She is the author of all the books and box sets in White Star Kids' Montessori: A World of Achievements series.

FEDERICA FUSI was born in Massa Marittima, in the province of Grosseto. Passionate about drawing since she was a child, she graduated from the arts high school in Grosseto. She continued her training at the Academy of Fine Arts in Florence, graduating with a diploma in decorative arts. She then went on to painting, specializing in visual arts and new expressive languages. She later specialized in illustration at the Nemo Academy of Digital Art in Florence. Federica currently lives in Florence, where she teaches and passionately pursues her career as a professional illustrator.

Published by DragonFruit, an imprint of Mango Publishing, a division of Mango Publishing Group, Inc.

Graphic design by Valentina Figus

Mango is an active supporter of authors' rights to free speech and artistic expression in their books. Thank you in advance for respecting our authors' rights. For permission requests, please contact the publisher at:
Mango Publishing Group
2850 Douglas Road, 4th Floor
Coral Gables, FL
33134 USA
info@mango.bz

For special orders, quantity sales, course adoptions and corporate sales, please email the publisher at sales@mango.bz. For trade and wholesale sales, please contact Ingram Publisher Services at customer.service@ingramcontent.com or +1.800.509.4887.

A First Book of Mindfulness for Kids
ISBN: (p) 978-1-68481-142-7 (e) 978-1-68481-143-4
BISAC: JNF024130JUVENILE, NONFICTION / Health & Daily Living / Mindfulness & Meditation

White Star Kids® is a registered trademark property of White Star s.r.l.

© 2020 White Star s.r.l.
Piazzale Luigi Cadorna, 6 - 20123 Milan, Italy
www.whitestar.it

Translation: TperTradurre, Rome
Editing: Leo Costigan

ISBN 978-88-544-1685-7
1 2 3 4 5 6   24 23 22 21 20

Printed in China